DATE			

BAKER & TAYLOR

SUPER SANDCASTLE™
Animal Habitats

What Lives in Coral Reefs?

Oona Gaarder-Juntti

Consulting Editor, Diane Craig, M.A./Reading Specialist

ABDO
Publishing Company

Credits
Editor: Liz Salzmann
Content Developer: Nancy Tuminelly
Cover and Interior Design and Production: Oona Gaarder-Juntti, Mighty Media
Illustration: Oona Gaarder-Juntti
Photo Credits: AbleStock, iStockphoto/Kathi Shotwell, Douglas Faulkner/Peter Arnold Inc., ShutterStock

Library of Congress Cataloging-in-Publication Data

Gaarder-Juntti, Oona, 1979-

What lives in coral reefs? / Oona Gaarder-Juntti.

p. cm. -- (Animal habitats)

ISBN 978-1-60453-170-1

1. Coral reef animals--Juvenile literature. 2. Coral reef ecology--Juvenile literature.
I. Title.

QL125.G23 2008

591.77'89--dc22

2008005476

Super SandCastle™ books are created by a team of professional educators, reading specialists, and content developers around five essential components—phonemic awareness, phonics, vocabulary, text comprehension, and fluency—to assist young readers as they develop reading skills and strategies and increase their general knowledge. All books are written, reviewed, and leveled for guided reading, early reading intervention, and Accelerated Reader® programs for use in shared, guided, and independent reading and writing activities to support a balanced approach to literacy instruction.

About SUPER SANDCASTLE™

Bigger Books for Emerging Readers
Grades K–4

Created for library, classroom, and at-home use, Super SandCastle™ books support and engage young readers as they develop and build literacy skills and will increase their general knowledge about the world around them. Super SandCastle™ books are part of SandCastle™, the leading PreK–3 imprint for emerging and beginning readers. Super SandCastle™ features a larger trim size for more reading fun.

Let Us Know
Super SandCastle™ would like to hear your stories about reading this book. What was your favorite page? Was there something hard that you needed help with? Share the ups and downs of learning to read. We want to hear from you! Send us an e-mail.

sandcastle@abdopublishing.com

Contact us for a complete list of SandCastle™, Super SandCastle™, and other nonfiction and fiction titles from ABDO Publishing Company.

www.abdopublishing.com • 8000 West 78th Street
Edina, MN 55439 • 800-800-1312 • 952-831-1632 fax

Coral reefs are found in warm, shallow ocean waters. They cover less than 1 percent of the ocean floor but are home to 25 percent of all ocean animals.

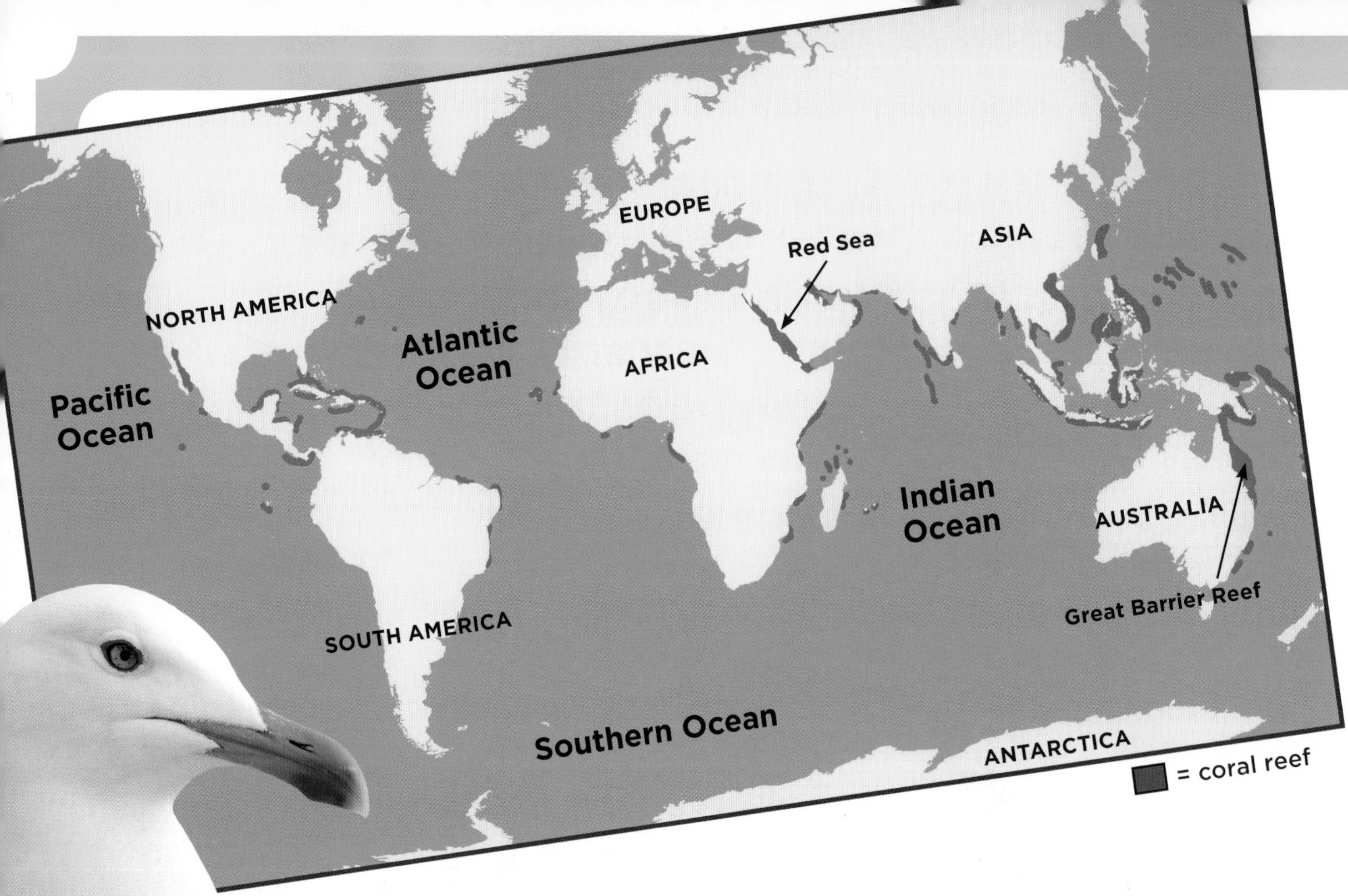
EUROPE
ASIA
Red Sea
NORTH AMERICA
Atlantic Ocean
AFRICA
Pacific Ocean
Indian Ocean
AUSTRALIA
Great Barrier Reef
SOUTH AMERICA
Southern Ocean
ANTARCTICA
= coral reef

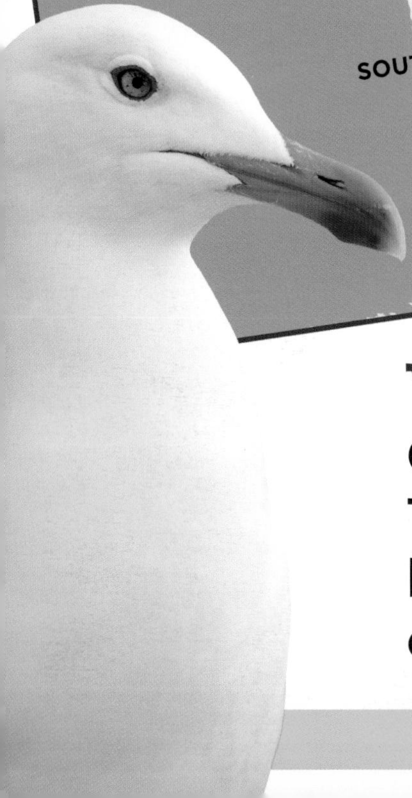

Where are coral reefs?

Coral reefs are located in tropical oceans. The Great Barrier Reef in Australia is the largest coral reef. Coral reefs help protect coastlines from ocean storms.

What do coral reefs look like?

A coral reef is made out of coral polyps. Coral polyps are tiny animals that form a colony attached to a large skeleton. When they die, the skeleton remains.

inner reef

a coral polyp

tentacle

mouth

limestone skeleton

reef crest

limestone

Dead coral forms the limestone base of the reef. New coral grows on the limestone.

outer reef

Christmas Tree Worm

Animal class: Invertebrate
Location: All tropical oceans

Christmas tree worms live in tubes that are attached to coral. They use their feathery tentacles for eating and breathing. They feed on tiny organisms that float by in the water.

Christmas tree worms can be many colors, including orange, blue, and pink. They are one to two inches long.

CLOWNFISH

Animal class: Fish
Location: Pacific Ocean, Indian Ocean, and Red Sea

Clownfish live among sea anemones. The tentacles of the sea anemones hide and protect the clownfish. Clownfish eat food scraps dropped by the sea anemones.

Clownfish help the sea anemones by cleaning them and driving away predators.

PUFFERFISH

Animal class: Fish
Location: Atlantic Ocean, Pacific Ocean, and Indian Ocean

Pufferfish get bigger when they feel threatened. They gulp water to make themselves twice their normal size. Pufferfish have spikes all over their bodies.

Many species of pufferfish have a poison in their bodies. The poison can hurt or kill their predators.

11

MORAY EEL

Animal class: Fish
Location: Pacific Ocean, Atlantic Ocean, and Indian Ocean

Moray eels hide in holes in the coral reef. They wait for prey to swim by and then they swallow the prey whole. Moray eels use their sense of smell to detect prey.

Moray eels keep their mouths open so water can flow through their gills.

BLUE-SPOTTED STINGRAY

Animal class: Fish
Location: Pacific Ocean and Red Sea

The blue-spotted stingray is green with bright blue spots. The spots warn predators that it is dangerous. It has a long tail with two poisonous stingers on the end.

The blue-spotted stingray has gills and a mouth on its underside.

Green Sea Turtle

Animal class: Reptile
Location: Pacific Ocean, Atlantic Ocean, and Indian Ocean

Green sea turtles are named for the greenish color of their fat. They can grow up to five feet long. They can weigh 300 to 400 pounds. Green sea turtles eat sea grasses and algae.

Female green sea turtles lay eggs on the beach where they were born.

MANATEE

Animal class: **Mammal**
Location: **Atlantic Ocean**

Manatees are nicknamed "sea cows." They are slow but graceful swimmers. They can grow 8 to 13 feet long and weigh up to 3,650 pounds. Manatees eat water plants.

A manatee can eat up to 10 percent of its body weight a day. For a 1,000-pound manatee that's 100 pounds of food a day!

GREY REEF SHARK

Animal class: Fish
Location: Pacific Ocean, Indian Ocean, and Red Sea

Grey reef sharks swim along the outer edges of the coral reef. They form schools and hunt for fish together. They feed on fish, squid, crabs, and lobster.

Grey reef sharks grow up to eight feet long. They are recognizable by their broad, rounded snouts.

Have you ever been to a coral reef?

More Coral Reef Animals

Can you learn about these coral reef animals?

angelfish

brain coral

crab

giant clam

grouper

leatherback
  sea turtle

lobster

nurse shark

oyster

parrotfish

sea anemone

sea horse

sea urchin

sponge

star fish

tiger shark

whale shark

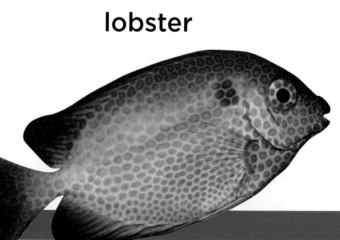

GLOSSARY

algae – a water plant such as seaweed.

dangerous – able or likely to cause harm or injury.

detect – to sense, discover, or find out about.

female – being of the sex that can produce eggs or give birth. Mothers are female.

gill – the organ on a fish's side that it breathes through.

invertebrate – a creature that does not have a spine.

outer – on the outside.

prey – an animal that is hunted or caught for food.

protect – to guard someone or something from harm or danger.

sea anemone – an invertebrate sea animal with brightly colored tentacles around its mouth.

snout – the projecting nose or jaws of an animal's head.

species – a group of related living beings.

tentacle – a long, flexible limb on an invertebrate such as a jellyfish, octopus, or squid.

threatened – to feel frightened by something.

tropical – located in the hottest areas on earth.